NATIONAL GEOGRAPHIC

D0503563

Going Up the Mountain

David Tunkin

Contents

The Base of the Mountain 5

The Mountain Forest 9

Above the Timberline 15

Above the Snowline 21

Glossary 24

This is a tall mountain.
Life at the top of the mountain is very different
from life at the base, or bottom, of the mountain.

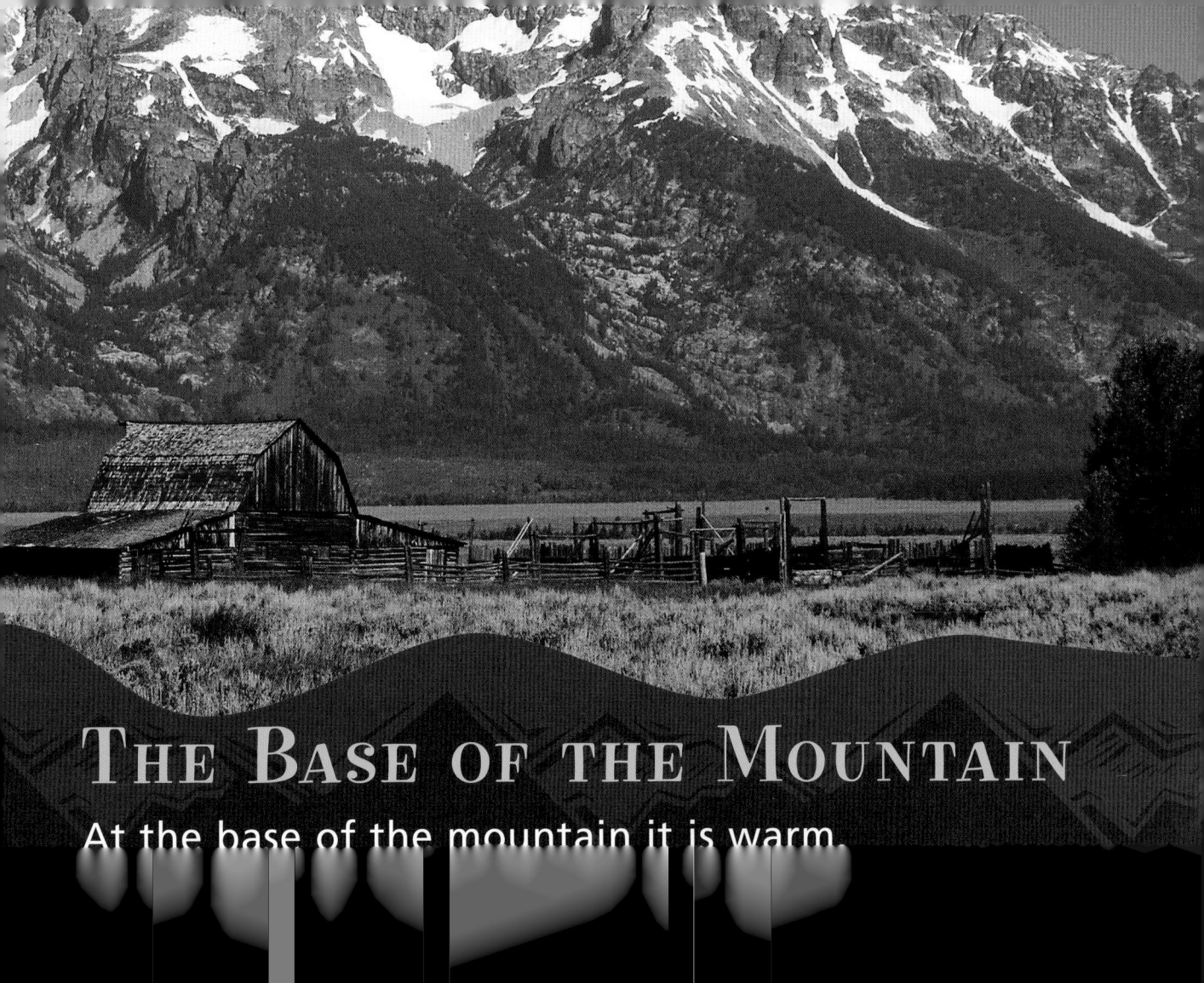

The Base of the Mountain

At the base of the mountain it is warm.

deer
rabbit

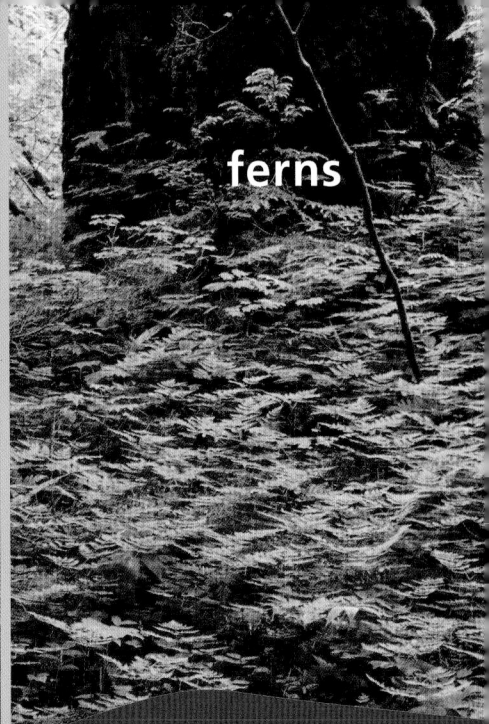

Many animals live at the base of the mountain.

Rabbits, deer, and badgers live here.

Many plants grow at the base of the mountain.

Flowers and ferns grow here.

The Mountain Forest

As you go up the mountain, it starts to get cooler.

Many trees grow in the forest here.

Evergreen and aspen trees grow thick and tall.

porcupine
beaver
snowshoe hare

Beavers, porcupines, and snowshoe hares all live in the mountain forest.

Wolves and bears live here, too.

woodpecker

Many birds live in the mountain forest.
Woodpeckers and owls live here.

Above the Timberline

As you go further up the mountain, it gets cooler still.

Soon there are no more trees.

This is called the timberline.

Trees do not grow above the timberline

moss

Mosses and grasses grow above the timberline.
They grow in mountain meadows.
Little flowers grow in the meadows in spring.

mountain goat

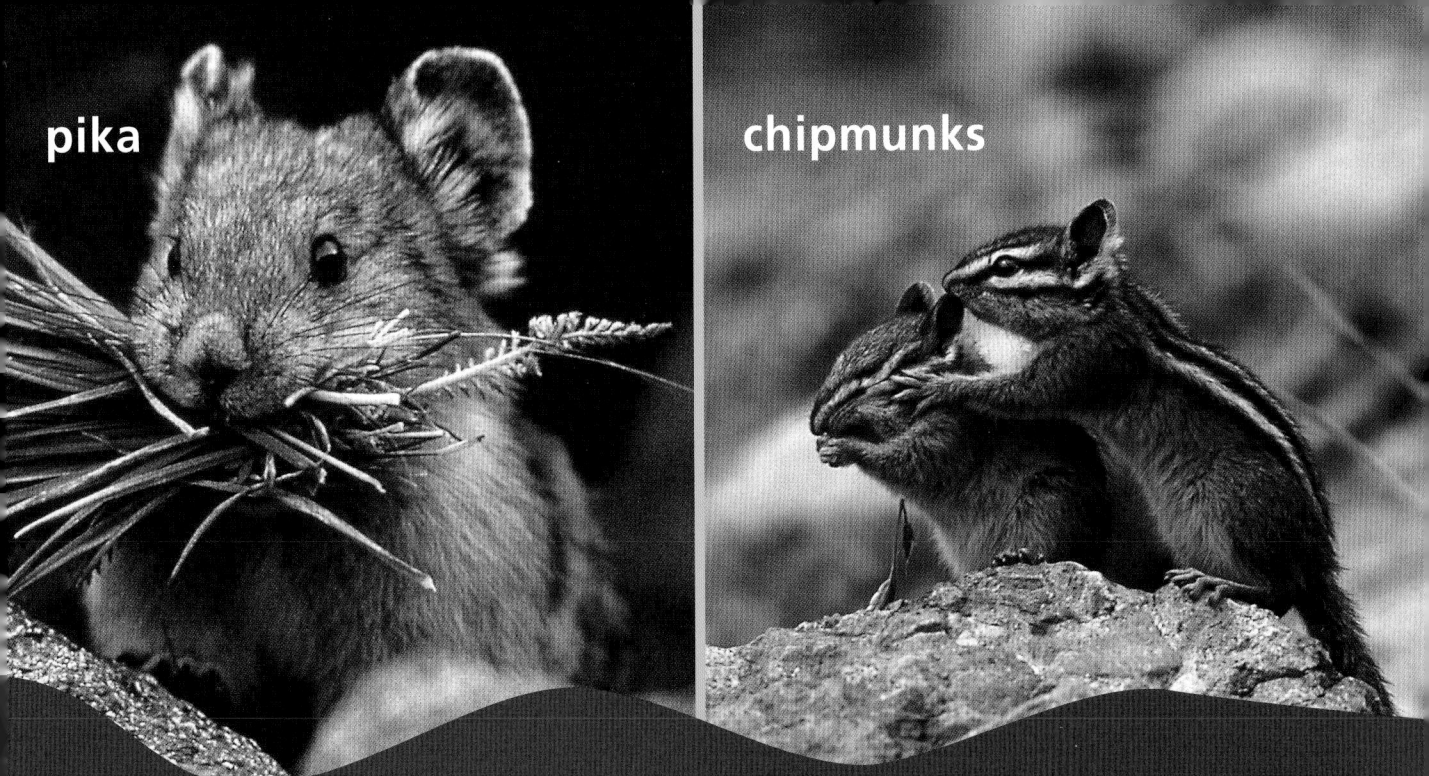

Different animals live above the timberline.
Mountain goats, pikas, and chipmunks all live here.

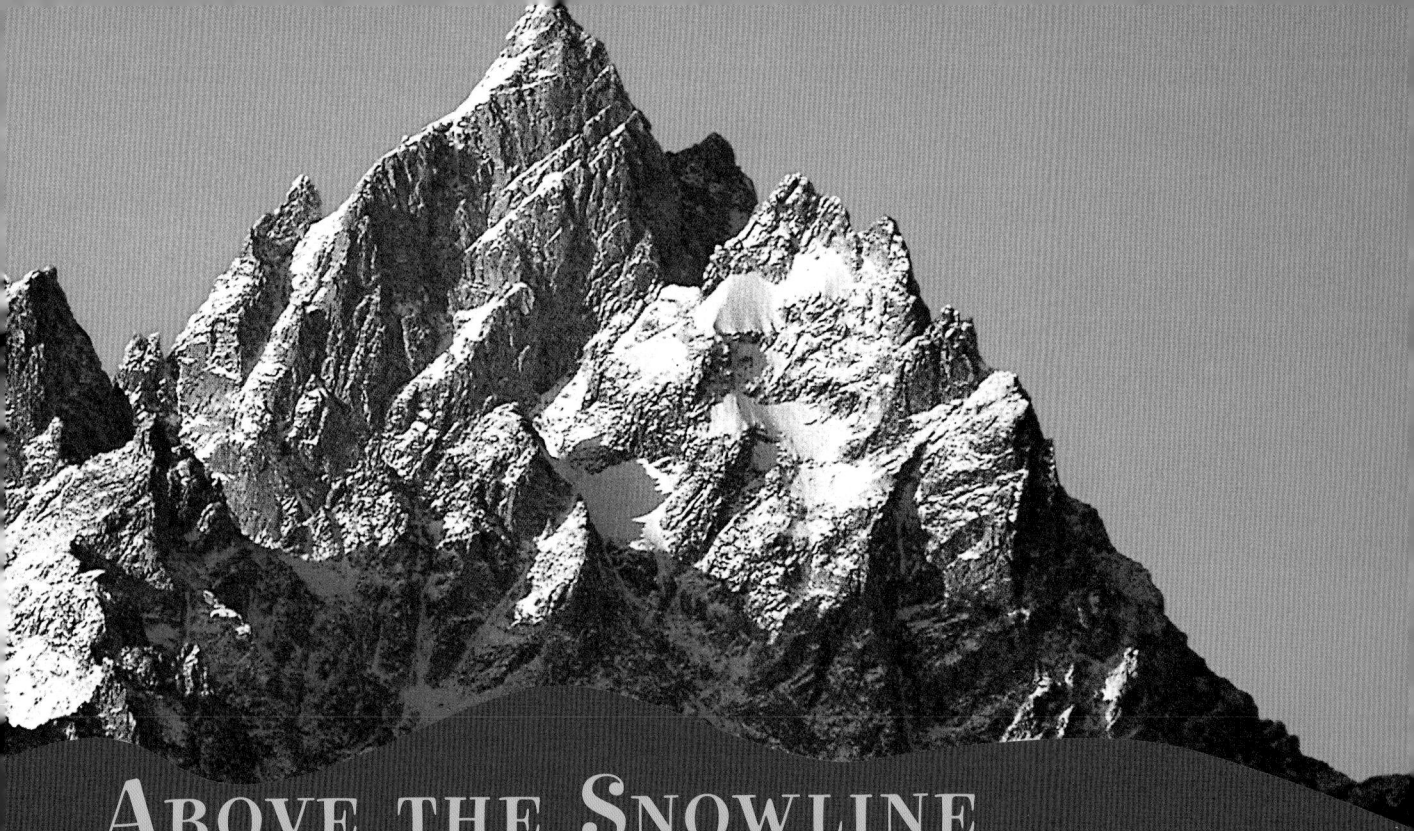

Above the Snowline

As you go further up the mountain, it gets colder. There is always ice and snow on the ground here.

Animals cannot live above the snowline.

Plants cannot grow here.

It is very cold and windy at the top of the mountain.

Glossary

fern	plant with feathery leaves and no flowers
forest	land covered with trees and other plants
meadow	land with grass on it
moss	plant that grows in damp places
mountain	very high hill
snowline	the line marking the area where ice and snow never melt on the top of a mountain
timberline	the line marking where trees stop growing on the side of a mountain